Sub-Saharan Africa

Lisa Zamosky

Publishing Credits

Associate Editor
Christina Hill, M.A.

Assistant Editor
Torrey Maloof

Editorial Assistants
Deborah Buchana
Kathryn R. Kiley
Judy Tan

Editorial Director
Emily R. Smith, M.A.Ed.

Editor-in-Chief
Sharon Coan, M.S.Ed.

Editorial Manager
Gisela Lee, M.A.

Creative Director
Lee Aucoin

Cover Designer
Lesley Palmer

Designers
Deb Brown
Zac Calbert
Amy Couch
Robin Erickson
Neri Garcia

Publisher
Rachelle Cracchiolo, M.S.Ed.

Teacher Created Materials

5301 Oceanus Drive
Huntington Beach, CA 92649
http://www.tcmpub.com
ISBN 978-0-7439-0438-4
© 2007 Teacher Created Materials, Inc.
Reprinted 2010
Printed in China

Table of Contents

The Big Continent

Africa is the second largest continent on Earth. It is bigger than all of the United States and Europe put together. Africa is located just south of Europe and southwest of the Middle East. The equator runs through the center of Africa.

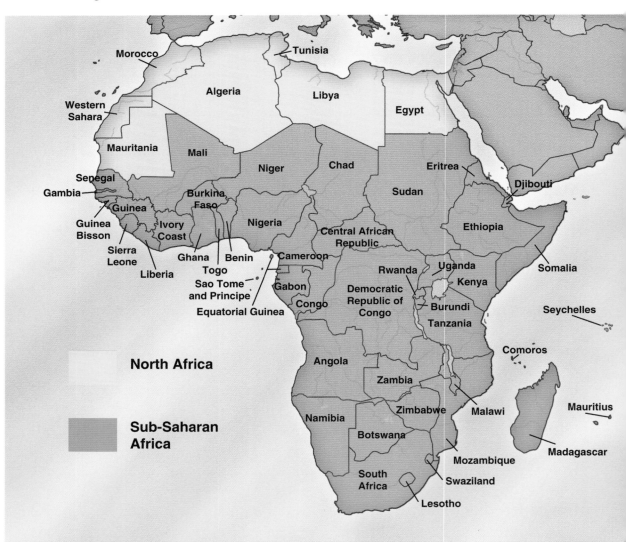

▲ Most of Africa is south of the Sahara Desert.

Africa is home to the Sahara (suh-HAWR-uh) Desert. The Sahara is the largest desert in the world. The area of land south of the Sahara Desert is called Sub-Saharan Africa. This region has many different types of **climates** and landforms. Grasslands, rain forests, and jungles can all be found there.

Over thousands of years, people from all over the world have come to Sub-Saharan Africa. They have shaped the **cultures** and customs of the land. This region of Africa has had a very long and complicated history.

Mount Kilimanjaro

Mount Kilimanjaro (kil-uh-muhn-JAWR-oh) is the highest mountain in all of Africa. The mountain is located in Tanzania (tan-zuh-NEE-uh).

The Nile River

The longest river in Africa is the Nile. In ancient times, the Egyptians (ih-JIP-shuhnz) relied on the Nile to survive. Today, Africans still depend upon its water for food, energy, and transportation.

▼ The Nile has been an important river for thousands of years.

Early African Farmers

Savannas (suh-VAN-nuhz) cover much of Africa. These are large areas of land covered with grass and trees. Savannas are the best type of land in Sub-Saharan Africa for farming.

Africans began farming over 4,000 years ago. To ready the land for planting, they would set fires to clear it of grass and trees. The crops were then planted in the ashes. Once the crops were **harvested** (HAWR-vuhst-ed), grass would grow back. Then, the grass would be ready to burn again the next year.

Grains such as millet (MIL-luht) and sorghum (SORE-guhm) were able to grow well in "savanna soil." Vegetables such as okra (OH-kruh), yams, and peas grew well, too. Farmers on the savannas also raised goats and cattle.

▲ This fire burns grass and bushes.

Fire in the Savanna

Using fire to manage the growth of savannas is still a common practice by farmers in Africa.

Traditional Ways

Although modern equipment is used to harvest wheat on the savannas of Kenya (KEN-yuh), women still grind grain by hand. This is just what they did thousands of years ago.

▲ African women grind grain by hand.

The Kingdom of Kush

One of the first **civilizations** (siv-uh-luh-ZAY-shuhnz) in northeastern Africa was a group of people called the Kush (KUHSH). The Kush ruled a part of Africa that is now in the country of Sudan (sue-DAN). The Kush civilization existed from about 1100 B.C. to A.D. 350.

Egyptian trade routes along the Nile River passed through the Kush kingdom. Ivory, ebony, and animal furs were traded along these routes. The Kush gained control of these routes and became very wealthy. They lived in beautiful palaces. They built grand temples and tombs that were shaped like pyramids.

▼ These are the ruins of Kush pyramids.

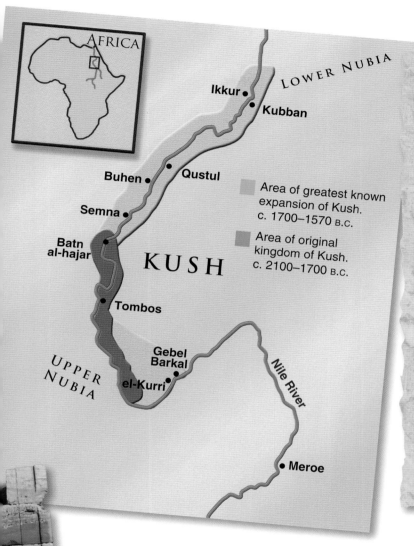

KUSH

LOWER NUBIA

Ikkur

Kubban

Buhen • Qustul

Semna •

Batn al-hajar

Tombos

Gebel Barkal

UPPER NUBIA

el-Kurri

Nile River

Meroe

AFRICA

Area of greatest known expansion of Kush. c. 1700–1570 B.C.

Area of original kingdom of Kush. c. 2100–1700 B.C.

Ancient Travel, Modern Records

Ancient Africans traveled a lot. Records today show that East African traders made it all the way to India.

Egyptian Influences

The Kush traded with the Egyptians for many years. During this time, the Kush were influenced by Egyptian culture. The Kush began to worship Egyptians gods. They even started using **hieroglyphics** (HI-ruh-glif-iks).

For 100 years, the Kush took over control of Egypt. They ruled Egypt until the Assyrians (uh-SEAR-ee-uhnz) conquered them. The Kush did not like losing to the Assyrians. The Assyrian weapons were stronger than the Kush's weapons. So, the Kush began making weapons and tools from iron. Soon, they were one of the largest iron-making civilizations in the world.

The Aksum Kingdom

The kingdom of Aksum came into power in the first century A.D. The Aksum traded **agriculture** (AG-rih-kuhl-chuhr), gold, and ivory along the coast of the Red Sea. They gained power by taking control of this trade route as well as others. **Merchants** traveling to the east passed through Aksum's port city of Adulis (AH-juh-luhs) on the Red Sea. This gave the Aksum rulers a connection to India, Egypt, and the Roman Empire. It brought the civilization great wealth.

The Aksum built many structures. They made their own coins out of gold, copper, and silver. Many of the coins were stamped with the Christian cross. Around A.D. 700, the Arabic (AIR-uh-bik) world took control of the trading routes in the region. Aksum was left out and lost its power.

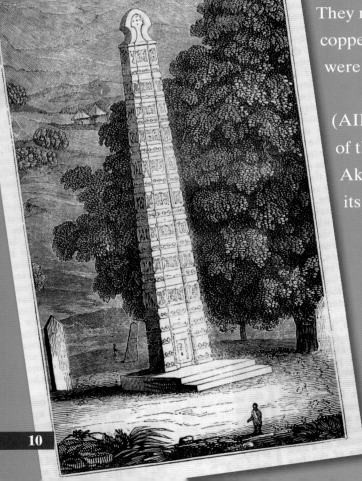

Ethiopia today ▶

◀ The Aksum people left behind artifacts that people study today.

◀ These children are carrying millet to market.

Old Crops

Millet, sorghum, okra, and peas are crops that are just as important to Africa today as they were 4,000 years ago.

Ancient Land

Aksum was located high in the mountains of modern-day Ethiopia (ee-thee-OH-pee-uh).

Christianity in Ethiopia

The Zagwe (ZAWG-way) dynasty started ruling Ethiopia in about A.D. 1137. Its rulers were nomads and soldiers. They were also very religious Christians. The Zagwe were dedicated to building monuments. Their monuments honored Christianity.

Their most powerful leader was King Lalibela (lah-lee-BEL-uh). He ruled Ethiopia from about A.D. 1185 to 1225. During his rule, eleven stone churches were created in the capital city. These churches were not built. They were actually carved right out of the stone.

The Amhara (am-HAR-uh) people lived to the south of the Zagwe. They were very powerful. The Amhara leader was Amlak (am-LAWK). He drove away the last Zagwe ruler around A.D. 1270. Then, he called himself the king of the area.

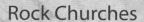
You can see how this church was carved from stone.

▼ The Lalibela churches are made completely from stone.

Rock Churches

The rock churches carved during the reign of King Lalibela can be seen today in Lalibela, Ethiopia.

Lasting Tradition

Christian churches in Ethiopia still follow traditions that were created under the Zagwe rulers.

Religious Tradition

Ethiopia is home to one of the oldest Christian churches in the world. Nearly half of all Ethiopians today are Christians.

The Empire of Ghana

Most of the world's gold came from West Africa. Beginning in the 700s, Muslim (MUHZ-luhm) traders started to trade gold. They traveled from North Africa to West Africa. To do so, they traveled through the Empire of Ghana (GAW-nuh).

Because the weather was so hot, West Africans needed a way to keep their food from going bad. Salt preserved food in the heat. But, West Africans could not make salt for themselves. The Muslims brought salt from the north in exchange for gold.

▼ This map shows ancient Ghana and Ghana today.

Morocco

Mauritania

Mali

Niger

Ancient
Ghana

Senegal

Burkina
Faso

Guinea

Ivory
Coast   Ghana

◀ Salt is still traded in Africa today.

Ghana controlled the major trade routes in Northwest Africa. They taxed the traders using the routes. They also controlled the amount of gold that was available to the market. This kept the supply of gold low. That meant that demand for gold was high. So, the prices stayed high. Ghana became a very wealthy civilization.

Around the middle of the 1000s, North Africans began to attack Ghana. The trade routes they controlled were too valuable. By 1230, Ghana had disappeared.

Salt Mining

Salt trade was very important in African countries long ago. This industry still exists in Mali (MAH-lee) and Niger (NI-juhr).

Important Iron

Iron was another important metal in Ghana's history. The people of Ghana used iron to make weapons. They created swords, daggers, and arrows to trade. These weapons made Ghana's army very powerful.

Ghana Today or Ghana Then?

The country of Ghana today is located south of where the Ghana Empire was originally located.

▼ Ghana today

The Rise of Mali

Mali gained power in the same way as the Empire of Ghana. It controlled trade routes across Africa. Mali was in the same region as Ghana. But, Mali was much larger than Ghana.

Sundiata (soon-JAH-tuh) was the first ruler of Mali. He made the salt-gold trade even more successful than before. He also built Niani (nih-AW-nih), which was the capital of ancient Mali. This city was near the major trade routes along the Niger River. Timbuktu (tim-buhk-TOO) was the cultural (KUHL-chuh-ruhl) center of Niani. The city was also the last stop for **caravans** heading across the Sahara Desert. Farmers came to Timbuktu to sell their crops in the markets. And, merchants traded their goods there.

Sundiata made an important decision for his empire. He chose to convert to Islam (is-LAWM). Once he became a Muslim, he was called Mansa Sundiata. The word *mansa* (MAHN-suh) means "emperor." All of the Mali rulers were Muslims. The most famous Mali ruler was Mansa Musa (MOO-suh).

◀ Huge salt pile in Mali

Still Trading

The trade that was strong between Africans and Arabs (AIR-uhbz) in Timbuktu continues today. Salt is still a very important trade item.

Mixed Buildings

Timbuktu still has both African- and Arab-style buildings. African buildings are rounded and Arab buildings are square in shape.

▼ A huge market sets up outside this Arab building in Mali.

◀ These camels are crossing the Sahara. Camels were the main form of transportation in the desert.

Mansa Musa

Mansa Musa controlled Mali from 1312–1337. During his rule, there were 40 to 50 million people within the empire. Mali was at the peak of its power during these years. Musa helped his empire grow in size, knowledge, and culture. He encouraged the arts, **architecture**, and literature.

Musa was a loyal Muslim. In 1324, he made a **pilgrimage** (PIL-gruhm-ij) to Mecca (MEK-kuh). Mecca is a holy city for Muslims. It is in current-day Saudi Arabia (SAW-dee uh-RAY-bee-uh). His trip

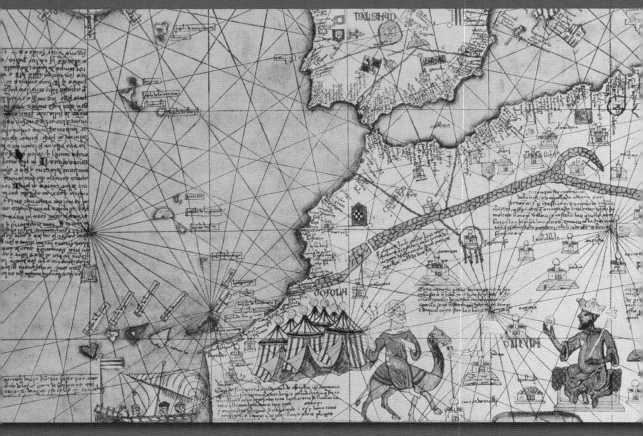

▲ This map shows Musa's trip to Mecca.

was called a *hajj* (HAJ). It is said that he traveled with thousands of people. He brought maids, musicians, teachers, and slaves. He also brought a lot of gold. He wanted to show how powerful Mali was by bringing along all of his riches. During his travels, he gave away many gifts.

After one year, he arrived at the holy city. Musa's pilgrimage made him very famous. It also opened up trade between Mali and the Arab world.

Remaining Mosque

Mansa Musa built palaces and a **mosque** (MAWSK) in Timbuktu. The mosque still exists today.

Beginning of Islam in Mali

The religion of Islam was very important to Musa. He encouraged scholars to come to Mali and teach about the religion. This region remains a center of Islamic culture today.

▼ Mecca's Great Mosque is a very holy site for Muslims.

The Songhai Empire

The Mali Empire came to an end by the 1400s. The Songhai (son-GAH-ee) Empire grew in its place. In fact, the Songhai Empire had been slowly coming to power for many years. It became even stronger than Mali.

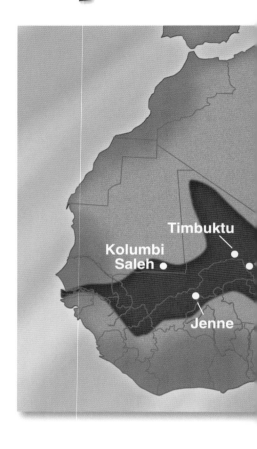

It remained powerful for about 100 years. King Sunni Ali Ber (SUN-nee aw-LEE BUHR) was one of this empire's strongest leaders. He expanded the kingdom to include Mali and other parts of West Africa.

Songhai kings had assistants called griots (GREE-ohz). Griots kept the empire's history alive. They told stories about events and cultural traditions. The griots' stories have been told again and again for thousands of years. Through this oral tradition, the stories of ancient empires live today.

The Moroccan (muh-RAW-kuhn) army attacked the Songhai Empire in 1591. Morocco's leader wanted complete control of West Africa and its gold mines. The Moroccan army was too strong for the Songhai. The Songhai Empire was defeated.

◀ These African griots tell a tale.

Gao

SONGHAI EMPIRE

Modern-Day Griots

Today in Africa, griots continue to tell stories of African history and tradition. Griots often know hundreds of historical stories by heart.

Saving Elephants

Ivory is taken from the tusk of an elephant. Today, killing elephants for ivory is illegal. That has not always been the case. Today, elephants are becoming endangered and must be protected.

▼ Ivory was very valuable.

Swahili People

Merchants sailed between Africa and Asia through the Indian Ocean. During that time, towns developed along the eastern coast of Africa. This is where merchants traded their goods. Africans sold gold, shells, animal skins, ivory, and human slaves. The Africans bought goods from Asia. They also bought from Persia (PURR-zhuh) and India.

A lot of the merchants coming to the cities on the coast of Africa were Arab Muslims. In time, many of them made these cities their homes. The Arab language and religion became a part of the culture along the coast. This coastal culture is known as Swahili (swaw-HEE-lee). The word *Swahili* means "people of the shore" in Arabic.

Islam became an important religion for many Africans living in the port cities in East Africa.

▲ This is a fruit market in Zanzibar, Tanzania.

Indian Ocean Trade Routes

Arabia

China

Japan

India and
Bengal

Sri
Lanka

Indonesia

Trade
with Europe

Trade within
Asia

New Name

The Swahili people had a city called Zanzibar (ZAN-zuh-bawr). It was on an island. Today, that island is part of the country of Tanzania.

Ports Still in Action

Old Swahili ports such as Mombasa (mawm-BAW-suh) and Zanzibar still ship goods around the world.

▲ Zanzibar seaport

Swahili and Its Cities

The Swahili cities gained control over the Indian Ocean trade routes. These cities became more powerful. As the wealth from trading grew, several towns along the eastern coast became very important.

The cities of Mombasa, Zanzibar, and Mogadishu (mawg-uh-DIH-shoo) were in the north. These cities traded iron, gold, and wood. Lamu (LAH-moo) and Kilwa (kil-WAH) were two other important Swahili port cities to the south. Swahili civilization was at its height between the thirteenth and fifteenth centuries.

Spices were valuable for traders. ▶

◀ Tortoise shells

◀ Natives of Kenya

Spice

In the 1400s, Zanzibar was known for ivory, tortoise shells, and other goods. Today, Zanzibar mainly produces spices such as nutmeg, cinnamon, and pepper.

Swahili Legacy

Swahili is still the language of Tanzania, Kenya, Zaire (ZI-yuhr), and Uganda (yu-GAWN-duh) today.

Changing Island

Mombasa was located on an island that is part of present-day Kenya.

Great Zimbabwe

There once was a great stone city in southern Africa. The architecture was very advanced. The walls and buildings were larger than any others in Africa at the time. Stones were created to fit together perfectly with no mortar. This city was called Great Zimbabwe (zim-BAW-bway). Sadly, the structures were destroyed. Only their ruins can be visited today.

The ruins of Great Zimbabwe indicate that it was a very wealthy culture. The people of the city traded with a southern Swahili town, Sofala (soo-faw-LAH). Although many different items were traded, gold was the most important. Some of the richest gold fields in southern Africa are around Zimbabwe. During the 1300s, the ruling families

▲ The ruins of Great Zimbabwe can be visited today.

increased the amount of gold mined for trading with Sofala. This made Zimbabwe very wealthy.

The community began to disappear around the late 1400s. The reasons for this are not known.

▼ Harare, Zimbabwe, today

▼ You can see how well these stones fit together.

Events of Yesterday Seen Today

The different cultures of Sub-Saharan Africa developed over thousands of years. Gold, ivory, and other trade goods made many of the civilizations very wealthy. As empires and cities gained control over trade routes, their power rose. When control of trade routes was lost, so was the power and wealth.

As communities came into contact with people from different parts of the world, their cultures were changed. New religions and traditions became a part of Africa. Arab Muslims made a big impact on Sub-Saharan Africa throughout its history. These influences and many others can still be seen throughout Africa today.

A city in ▶
Ghana today

◀ Some Africans still follow ancient traditions.

European Colonies

Starting in the 1400s, Europeans (yur-uh-PEE-uhnz) started setting up trading posts in Africa. By the 1800s, Europeans were moving to the continent. They set up colonies there. The Europeans wanted the valuable natural resources. By 1914, only two areas of Africa were free.

Ending Colonization

In the 1950s, some African countries started to gain independence. But, it was not until 1980 that the last country was finally free.

Glossary

agriculture—having to do with farming; producing crops and raising animals

architecture—the process of making plans for buildings

caravans—lines of people traveling together

civilizations—societies that have writing and keep track of records

climates—general weather patterns of a region

cultures—people's ways of life, including art, religion, music, and language

descendents—relatives from long ago

harvested—gathered crops

hieroglyphics—pictures or symbols representing words, syllables, or sounds; used by the ancient Egyptians instead of alphabetical writing

merchants—people who sell goods for money

mosque—Muslim building for worship

pilgrimage—a journey to a sacred place

Index

Image Credits

cover Photos.com; p.1 Photos.com; p.4 The Library of Congress Geography and Map Division; p.5 Paul Cowan/Shutterstock, Inc.; p.6 AfriPics.com; p.7 (top) blickwinkel/Alamy; p.7 (bottom) AfriPics.com; p.8 age fotostock/SuperStock; p.9 (top) Teacher Created Materials; p.10 Mary Evans Picture Library/Alamy; p.11 (top) Andrew Watso/Alamy; p.11 (bottom) Jan Martin Will/Shutterstock, Inc.; p.12 Ariadne Van Zandbergen/Alamy; p.13 (left) Martin Gray/Getty Images; p.13 (right) Charles Taylor/Shutterstock, Inc.; p.14 Teacher Created Materials; p.15 (top) Andrew Watson/Alamy; p.15 (bottom) Theunis Jacobus Botha/Shutterstock, Inc.; p.16 age fotostock/SuperStock; p.17 (top) Jose Fuente/Shutterstock, Inc.; p.17 (bottom) Gary Cook/Alamy; p.18 The Granger Collection, New York; p.19 Shamsul bin Fitri/Shutterstock, Inc.; p.20 Teacher Created Materials; p.21 (top) Black Star/Alamy; p.21 (bottom left) The Library of Congress; p.21 (bottom right) Chris Fourie/Shutterstock, Inc.; p.22 The Library of Congress; p.23 (top) Teacher Created Materials; p.23 (bottom) James Strachan/Getty Images; pp.24–25 Cecilia Lim H M/Shutterstock, Inc.; p.25 (left) Photos.com; p.25 (right) Vera Bogaerts/Shutterstock, Inc.; p.26 Images of Africa Photobank/Alamy; p.27 (top) Lakis Fourouklas/Shutterstock, Inc.; p.27 (bottom) Sylvia Cordaiy Photo Library Ltd./Alamy; pp.28–29 Kondrachov Vladimir/Shutterstock, Inc.; p.29 (top) Jeff Schultes/Shutterstock, Inc.; p.29 (bottom) Afripics.com; back cover iStockphoto.com/Alan Tobey